W9-BEE-246

Explore Saturn

Liz Milroy

Lerner Publications • Minneapolis

Scan the QR code on page 21 to see Saturn in 3D!

Lerner Publications Company
An imprint of Lerner Publishing Group, Inc.
241 First Avenue North
Minneapolis, MN 55401 USA

For reading levels and more information, look up this title at www.lernerbooks.com.

Main body text set in Billy Infant regular.
Typeface provided by SparkType.

Editor: Brianna Kaiser **Photo Editor:** Brianna Kaiser

Library of Congress Cataloging-in-Publication Data

Names: Milroy, Liz, author.
Title: Explore Saturn / Liz Milroy.
Other titles: Lightning bolt books. Planet explorer.
Description: Minneapolis, MN : Lerner Publications, 2021 | Series: Lightning bolt books—Planet explorer | Includes bibliographical references and index. | Audience: Ages 6-9 | Audience: Grades 2-3 | Summary: "Learn about Saturn's vast and beautiful network of rings, and see how it is similar to or different from other planets. Updated scientific discoveries accompany this lively text for beginning readers"— Provided by publisher.
Identifiers: LCCN 2020017757 (print) | LCCN 2020017758 (ebook) | ISBN 9781728404134 (library binding) | ISBN 9781728423654 (paperback) | ISBN 9781728418490 (ebook)
Subjects: LCSH: Saturn (Planet)—Juvenile literature.
Classification: LCC QB671 .M55 2021 (print) | LCC QB671 (ebook) | DDC 523.46—dc23

LC record available at https://lccn.loc.gov/2020017757
LC ebook record available at https://lccn.loc.gov/2020017758

Manufactured in the United States of America
1-48471-48985-6/9/2020

Table of Contents

All about Saturn

You're flying past amazing rings. You're on Saturn! It's the second-largest planet in our solar system.

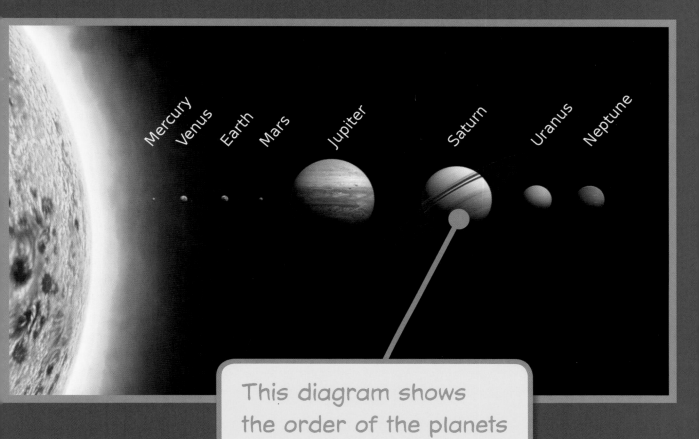

Mercury Venus Earth Mars Jupiter Saturn Uranus Neptune

This diagram shows the order of the planets in the solar system.

Saturn is the sixth planet in the solar system. It's about 886 million miles (1.4 billion km) away from the sun.

Saturn is called a gas giant. Like Jupiter, it is really big and made mostly of gas. If you could find an ocean large enough to hold Saturn, Saturn's gas would make the planet float.

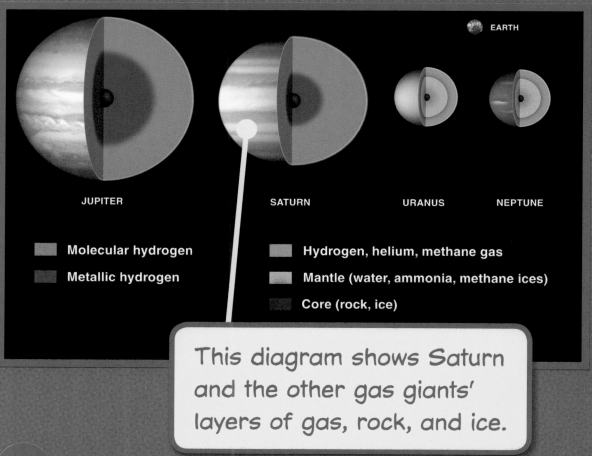

EARTH

JUPITER

SATURN

URANUS

NEPTUNE

Molecular hydrogen

Metallic hydrogen

Hydrogen, helium, methane gas

Mantle (water, ammonia, methane ices)

Core (rock, ice)

This diagram shows Saturn and the other gas giants' layers of gas, rock, and ice.

This image shows how large Saturn is compared to Earth.

Saturn is about 75,000 miles (120,000 km) across. Nine Earths could line up across Saturn. If Earth were as big as a nickel, Saturn would be the size of a volleyball.

Rings and Moons of Saturn

Saturn is visible in the night sky even without a telescope. It looks like a bright yellow star. But Saturn's rings can't be seen without using at least a small telescope.

Saturn's rings are made up of ice and rock. The rings are 170,000 miles (273,600 km) wide.

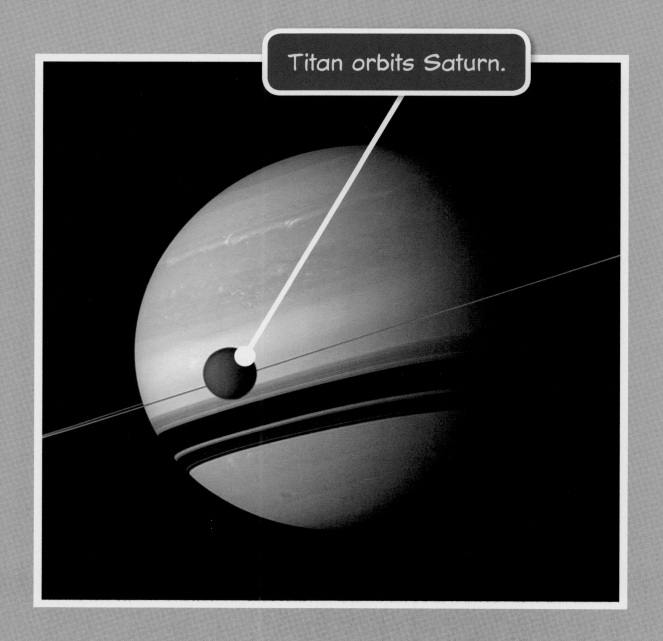

Astronomers have proven that Saturn has at least eighty-two moons. Astronomers are studying them.

Titan, Saturn's largest moon, has its own atmosphere. This is not common for a moon.

Titan is the second-largest moon in the solar system.

Living on Saturn

On Saturn, days are short but years are long. A day is less than eleven hours, but a year on Saturn is twenty-nine Earth years.

This image shows a storm at Saturn's north pole. The image was taken by the *Cassini* spacecraft.

Earth has seasons because it is tilted on an axis. Saturn's tilt is similar to Earth's, so it also has seasons.

Saturn wouldn't be a nice place to visit. It doesn't have enough oxygen for you to breathe, and it is very cold. The average temperature on Saturn is −288°F (−178°C).

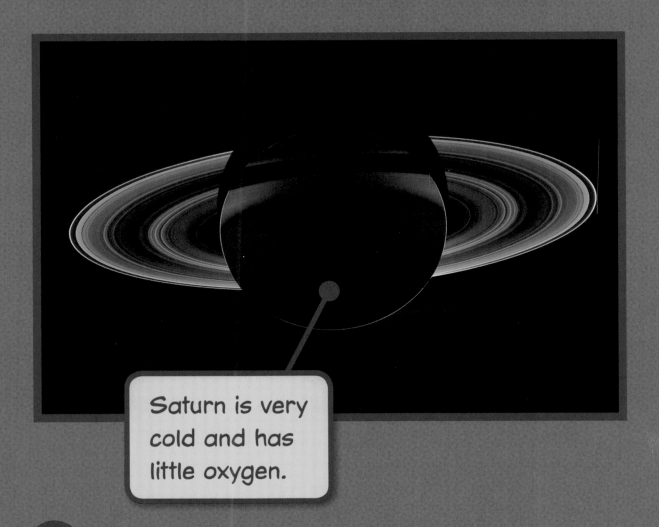

Saturn is very cold and has little oxygen.

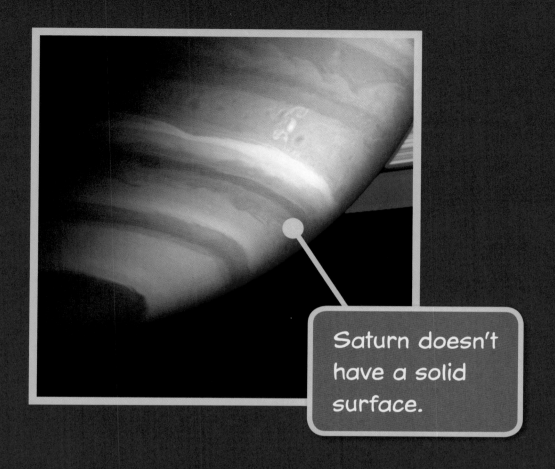

Saturn doesn't have a solid surface.

Since Saturn is made mostly of gas, it doesn't have a solid surface. A spacecraft wouldn't be able to land there, and Saturn's extreme temperatures and pressure would crush the spacecraft.

Checking Out Saturn

Four spacecraft have visited or flown past Saturn. *Pioneer 11* left Earth in 1973. It was the first to explore Saturn's rings.

Cassini flies near Saturn's atmosphere.

Cassini entered Saturn's orbit in 2004. It stayed in Saturn's orbit for thirteen years. It sent back important data on Saturn's weather and moons before the mission ended in 2017.

Titan also had a visitor. The *Huygens* probe landed there in 2005. It studied Titan's atmosphere and found lakes and rivers on its surface.

There is so much more to discover in space.

Future missions could check out more of Saturn's moons. Could people visit them someday? Maybe you'll help find out!

Planet Facts

- Saturn spins so fast that it bulges at the equator. This makes it look like a slightly squashed ball.

- Saturn is so far away from the sun that sunlight has to travel for seventy-nine minutes to reach it. That same light takes fewer than nine minutes to reach Earth.

- Saturn is named after the Roman god Saturnus. He was the god of agriculture and harvest.

Space Story

Every once in a while, Saturn will look as if it has no rings at all. This happens when Saturn and Earth line up in just the right way that only the very edge of Saturn's rings are visible from Earth. This makes the rings very hard to see, even with a strong telescope.

Scan the QR code to the right to see Saturn in 3D!

Glossary

astronomer: a scientist who looks at stars, planets, and other things in outer space

atmosphere: a layer of gas that surrounds a planet

axis: an invisible line that Saturn turns around

gas giant: a big planet that is made up mostly of gas

orbit: the path taken by one body circling around another body

solar system: our sun and everything that orbits around it

spacecraft: a ship made by people to move through space

telescope: a tool used to get a better look at objects in space

Learn More

Beth, Georgia. *Discover Saturn*. Minneapolis: Lerner Publications, 2019.

Milroy, Liz. *Explore Mercury*. Minneapolis: Lerner Publications, 2021.

NASA for Students
https://nasa.gov/stem/forstudents/k-4/index.html

NASA Space Place: All about Saturn
https://spaceplace.nasa.gov/all-about-saturn/en/

Nichols, Michelle. *Astronomy Lab for Kids: 52 Family-Friendly Activities*. Beverly, MA: Quarry, 2016.

Ready, Jet, Go! Planets in Our Solar System
https://pbskids.org/learn/readyjetgo/

Index

Photo Acknowledgments

Image credits: NASA/JPL/Space Science Institute, pp. 4, 7, 15; NASA/GSFC/SOHO/ESA (CC BY 2.0), p. 5; NASA/Lunar and Planetary Institute, p. 6; NASA/Jay Westcott, p. 8; NASA/MSFC, p. 9; NASA/GSFC, p. 10; NASA/JPL/University of Arizona/University of Idaho, p. 11; NASA/JPL-Caltech/Space Science Institute, pp. 12, 13, 14; NASA/ARC, p. 16; NASA/JPL-Caltech, pp. 17, 18; NASA/JPL/KSC, p. 19.

Cover: MarcelC/Getty Images.